GOOGLE

ABDO
Publishing Company

TECHNOLOGY
PIONEERS

GOOGLE

THE COMPANY AND ITS FOUNDERS

by Susan E. Hamen

Content Consultant
Jeffrey Barlow, PhD
Director, Berglund Center for Internet Studies
Pacific University

CREDITS

Published by ABDO Publishing Company, 8000 West 78th Street, Edina, Minnesota 55439. Copyright © 2011 by Abdo Consulting Group, Inc. International copyrights reserved in all countries. No part of this book may be reproduced in any form without written permission from the publisher. The Essential Library™ is a trademark and logo of ABDO Publishing Company.

Printed in the United States of America,
North Mankato, Minnesota
112010
012011

Editor: Melissa York
Copy Editor: Rebecca Rowell
Interior Design and Production: Kazuko Collins
Cover Design: Emily Love

Library of Congress Cataloging-in-Publication Data
Hamen, Susan E.
 Google : the company and its founders / by Susan E. Hamen.
    p. cm.
 Includes bibliographical references and index.
 ISBN 978-1-61714-808-8
 1. Google (Firm) 2. Internet industry—United States—History.
3. Web search engines—United States—History. I. Title.
 HD9696.8.U64G6653 2011
 338.7'6102504—dc22
                                    2010037884

TABLE OF CONTENTS

The graduate school partnership of Sergey Brin, *top*, and Larry Page led to the creation of Google.

HUMBLE BEGINNINGS

In 1997, two young Stanford University students knew they were onto something special. The pair had been working on a project that looked promising. If successful, it could revolutionize how people searched for information on the Internet—

and potentially bring huge changes to the Internet itself.

Sergey Brin and Larry Page, graduate students in computer science, were brilliant young prodigies who excelled at mathematics and engineering. Their minds never seemed to rest. While studying for their PhDs, they turned their interests toward creating a faster, easier, and better way of finding information in cyberspace.

In 1996, Brin and Page began working on a research project for the Stanford Digital Library Project (SDLP). The project involved developing technology for an integrated online library of information. It was the catalyst for one of the most important breakthroughs of the information age.

THE "SEARCH"

In the 1990s, the Internet was fairly new to the public. A world of possibilities had been opened, but finding information on the Internet was difficult. A person had to know the exact uniform resource locator, or URL, of a Web page. Otherwise, there was no guarantee he or she would find the location with a search. In August 1995, more than 18,000 Web sites existed, and that number was growing

THE WORLD WIDE WEB

The terms *Internet* and *World Wide Web* are often used interchangeably. However, the two are not the same thing. The Internet is the global data communications system that connects computers. The World Wide Web is a collection of interlinked documents that resides on the Internet. These documents appear as Web sites. A user can view Web pages using a Web browser. There are several browsers, including Internet Explorer, Firefox, Google Chrome, and Safari.

In 1989, British computer scientist Tim Berners-Lee proposed a system that would allow computer users to connect information of various kinds over a massive web. Berners-Lee was joined by Belgian computer scientist Robert Cailliau. The men proposed using hypertext, along with the Internet, to create their weblike system. Hypertext is a computer language that uses hyperlinks. A computer user needs only to click a hyperlink to go to a new Web page.

Berners-Lee developed the uniform resource locator (URL). A URL serves as a Web site's unique address on the World Wide Web. A user can find a certain Web site by knowing the URL or performing a search. The first Web site was created by Berners-Lee and described the World Wide Web project. It was put online on August 6, 1991.

daily. By 2006, that number would hit a milestone: 100 million. With an average of more than 9 million new Web sites created yearly, sifting through Web content to find useful information was a time-consuming challenge. Brin and Page knew the Internet held a vast amount of data. And they knew the data was useless if people could not find it easily.

Early search engines attempted to help users locate sites based on a search term. A person simply entered the word or words describing what he or she was trying to find, such as *dolphin* or *race cars*. Search engines such as WebCrawler, Lycos, Infoseek, and Excite worked by scanning Web sites for the search term entered. These early search engines produced a list of Web sites based on how many times the search term appeared on the Web page. None of the existing search engines provided a results list based on the quality of the Web site or the relevancy of the information. If a person conducted a search on dolphins, for example, he or she might get a list of several Web pages containing the word *dolphin*, but the results were not arranged in a helpful order. Simply because the word *dolphin* appeared more times on a Web page did not mean that page offered better information than another. These results, Brin and Page realized, were inefficient.

Page became interested in links on Web pages and how they might offer a new approach to searching. Links connect Web sites. A visitor to one site is sent to another by simply clicking

THE FIRST WEB SEARCH ENGINE

By 1990, many colleges and universities were using the Internet to store research papers and technical specifications. Although these were accessible to the public, unless a person knew the exact file name, it was virtually impossible to find these documents. McGill University student Alan Emtage created the first Internet search engine in 1990 to search these archives. Archie, as it was called, was a rudimentary solution to rummaging through archived material, only taking into account documents' titles, not their full text.

a highlighted word or phrase. Typically, the creator of a site provides links he or she feels are valuable to visitors to the site.

The pages linking to a Web site are called back links. A Web site does not necessarily have links to its back-linked pages. Graduate student Page believed links were similar to citations in published scholarly papers. When researching and writing, scientists cite, or reference, other published papers that support their ideas. Citations serve as a way of giving credit to other researchers for their work. By citing another person's work, a researcher is saying that the other work is useful or important.

Page explained, "Citations are important. It turns out, people who win the Nobel Prize have citations from 10,000 different papers." Page went on to explain that having many citations in scientific literature, "means your work was important, because other people thought it was worth mentioning."[1] Page wondered if he could apply the same logic to

Internet links. He applied this theory by suggesting that Internet sites with the most links to them were more important than sites with fewer links, as judged by Internet users. He also believed a back link with more back links to it carried more clout than one with fewer. If Page could follow back links on the Web, he could assign value to each Web site.

A PARTNERSHIP BLOOMS

Encouraged by Professor Terry Winograd, Page turned his idea into a PhD thesis. By this time, fellow student and friend Sergey Brin had joined Page on the project. They began working on their idea in January 1996. Page told one of his advisers his research would require him to download the entire World Wide Web onto his desktop computer in order to analyze the data. Many colleagues thought Page's idea was absurd.

With Brin's help, Page created a search engine he called BackRub to follow back links on the Internet. The young men needed an algorithm—a complex mathematical formula—to analyze

"It wasn't that [Brin and Page] sat down and said, 'Let's build the next great search engine.' They were trying to solve interesting problems and stumbled upon some neat ideas."[3]

—*Rajeev Motwani, Stanford University computer science professor*

OTHER FAMOUS ALGORITHMS

PageRank, the algorithm that led to Google, has become one of the most famous algorithms to date. Other algorithms have also changed everyday life for people worldwide. Encryption is an algorithmic process that makes text messages unreadable until they reach their destinations. Encryption also protects medical, financial, and other private information sent online.

Another famous algorithm is the MP3 file, which condenses music, decreasing it from the size of the recording in CD form while maintaining its quality. Music lovers can condense their entire audio library to the size of an MP3 player.

the back links. Brin created an algorithm with more than 500 million variables. The men named their algorithm PageRank, utilizing Page's last name.

Now, the pair needed to copy and index Web sites. This would require large numbers of computers working around the clock. The students were convinced they could recreate how people search for information online if they had the right equipment. If they could get their search engine up and running for use at Stanford, Brin and Page could prove its worth.

They began scavenging for extra computers and running PageRank. Soon, their project would outgrow their office at Stanford. Although Brin and Page had faith in their work, they probably had no idea they were on the verge of making history. +

Page studied links and back links to create a new method
for Internet searching.

Sergey Brin immigrated to the United States from Russia when he was six.

SERGEY BRIN

Sergey Mikhailovich Brin was born on August 21, 1973, in Moscow, Russia, when Russia was still a part of the Soviet Union. Young Sergey lived in a small, cramped apartment with his parents and grandmother. The only space

Sergey could play was in a small courtyard. The Brin family was Jewish and faced additional problems besides their living conditions.

At the time, Jews in the Soviet Union experienced anti-Semitism, or discrimination and hatred toward Jews. The government placed restrictions on what Jews could study in school. Sergey's father, Michael, had dreamed of becoming an astronomer. But Communist Party leaders barred Jews from studying physics. Since astronomy was a division of physics, Michael Brin had to abandon his dreams of studying the stars.

Nevertheless, Michael attended Moscow State University and studied mathematics. He graduated with honors and wanted to continue his studies, but explained, "Nobody would even consider me for graduate school because I was Jewish. That was normal."[1] He went to work as an

THE SOVIET UNION

The Soviet Union existed from 1922 until 1991. It included the areas that became Russia, Ukraine, and other eastern European and central Asian countries. The Soviet Union was ruled by its Communist Party. The ideology of communism called for the government to control the economy. The leaders controlled most aspects of the people's lives, including businesses, schools and universities, and the media. Many people lived in poor, tightly packed housing and faced shortages of basic goods. People were not allowed to speak out against the government. Many people, including Jews, were discouraged from practicing their religion.

economist and continued studying mathematics by sneaking into evening university seminars. He wrote several research papers, many of which were published, and began to work on a doctoral thesis. Mentors helped him find a university that would hear his thesis, and he received a PhD from a university in Kharkov, Ukraine, giving him a small raise in salary.

Sergey's mother, Eugenia, also attended Moscow State University. She received a degree from the School of Mechanics and Mathematics and worked in a laboratory at the Soviet Oil and Gas Institute.

Sergey's parents held respectable jobs, and they enjoyed conditions that were better than many others had living in Moscow at the time. However, Michael knew they would continue to suffer from anti-Semitism and his son would face the same educational restrictions he had.

RISKING EVERYTHING

When Sergey's parents applied for an emigration permit in 1978, his father was fired from his job. His mother was forced to quit hers. For many months, they struggled to get by on the money Michael made translating English technical documents into Russian. When their application was finally approved by the Soviet government, the family had to leave almost all of their possessions behind. They were some of the last Jews to leave Russia before the government ended emigration for a time.

Sergey received his first computer, a Commodore 64, when he was nine.

A BETTER LIFE AWAITS

After attending a mathematics conference in Warsaw, Poland, Michael returned home and told his wife and his mother, "We cannot stay here any more."[2] While at the conference, he met mathematicians from the United States, France, Germany, and Great Britain. He learned a little about what life could be like outside the Soviet Union. He was convinced his family could have a much better life in the West.

In 1979, when Sergey was six years old, his parents decided to immigrate to the United States. On October 25, the Brins landed in New York. The family included Michael, Eugenia, young Sergey, and

Michael's mother. With the help of the local Jewish community, the Brin family found a house to rent in Maryland, close to Washington DC, and Michael found work as a professor at the University of Maryland. Sergey's younger brother, Sam, was born in Maryland in 1988.

SERGEY THE STUDENT

Sergey attended the Miskan Torah Hebrew School with other Jewish children, but he disliked his school. He was a shy child who struggled to learn English and had a heavy accent. He was bullied by his classmates. After a few years, he begged his parents to allow him to transfer to a different school. Sergey was then enrolled in Paint Branch Montessori School in Adelphi, Maryland. The Montessori school allowed children to learn by doing things that interested them. Sergey spent most of his time doing puzzles, maps, and mathematics games. With the freedom to choose his own activities, Sergey's creativity grew. "I could grow at my own pace," he explained.[3] The Montessori school's methods taught Sergey he could learn through his curiosity for things that struck his fancy. He also did not face bullying at his new school.

BOY GENIUS

Sergey's parents stressed the importance of doing well in school. Both Sergey and his younger brother knew their parents expected them to excel and eventually earn PhDs. When Sergey was nine years old, his father gave him a Commodore 64 computer, which fueled his scientific and mathematical brain. Within a few years, his teachers realized the boy was a mathematical prodigy.

Sergey attended Eleanor Roosevelt High School in Greenbelt, Maryland, for just three years, while simultaneously earning

STANFORD UNIVERSITY

Stanford University is the birthplace of such groundbreaking computer companies as Hewlett-Packard, Sun Microsystems, Yahoo!, Cisco Systems, and Google. It has become synonymous with excellence in technology.

In 1876, Leland Stanford, a former California governor and a wealthy railroad businessman, purchased 650 acres (263 ha) of land south of the San Francisco area. He eventually purchased more land, for a total of more than 8,000 acres (3238 ha). A little town developed in the area. It was called Palo Alto, which means "tall tree" in Spanish and was named after a giant California redwood tree. The tree, now 1,070 years old, still stands and is Stanford University's symbol.

Leland Stanford and his wife, Jane, had one son, Leland Jr., who died at the age of 15. The grieving Stanfords founded Leland Stanford Junior University, better known as Stanford University, as a way to memorialize their son. They decided the university would be coeducational, admitting both female and male students. In its first year, a faculty of 15 served 559 students—a future president, Herbert Hoover, was one of the students. In 2009–2010, Stanford enrolled approximately 6,600 undergraduate students and 11,800 graduate students.

one year's worth of college credits. He had evolved from a shy child into an outspoken, confident, and sometimes cocky young man who was not afraid to challenge his teachers when he thought they were wrong. He often felt he received a better education at home from his parents than he did from his teachers.

Sergey began college math courses at the age of 15 at the University of Maryland and went on to complete a double major in mathematics and computer science. Finding his college courses no more difficult than his high school courses, Sergey finished in three years. He graduated with honors in 1993 at the age of 19.

Upon completing his undergraduate work, Sergey was awarded a prestigious National Science Foundation Scholarship. He was excited at the thought of attending Stanford University in California. In addition to the beautiful campus and the warm California weather, Sergey was pleased with the school's proximity to Silicon Valley, an area flourishing with high-tech entrepreneurs. Sergey was confident that pursuing his doctorate at Stanford would be a wise decision. He surely had no idea how that decision would affect his life. +

H.J. PATTERSON HALL

Sergey graduated from the University of Maryland
at College Park at age 19.

Larry Page has had a lifelong interest in technology and computers.

LARRY PAGE

Born on March 26, 1973, in East Lansing, Michigan, Lawrence Edward Page was the second son of Carl Victor Page and Gloria Page. Like his future partner Brin, Larry also had parents who placed a high value on scholarship.

Larry's father earned one of the first PhDs awarded in computer science and taught at Michigan State University. His mother taught computer programming classes at Michigan State as well. Larry was raised to excel in the world of computers and technology.

EARLY EXPOSURE

In a time when it was rare for families to have a home computer, the Pages had remarkable exposure to computing technology. Larry described his family's computer situation:

> *My dad was a computer science professor, so we had computers really early. The first computer we owned as a family was in 1978 [Larry would have been five years old], the Exidy Sorcerer. It was popular in Europe but never in the US. It had 32K memory. My brother had to write the operating system.*[1]

Larry's only brother, Carl Jr., was nine years older than Larry. Carl Jr. played a key role in teaching young Larry about computers and electronics. Carl Jr. attended Michigan State and brought home college-level electronics assignments that Larry worked on as an elementary school

FAMILY OF ENTREPRENEURS

Larry's brother did more than teach him to tinker with family appliances. Carl Jr. was the first entrepreneur in the family. After graduating from college, he cofounded an e-mail management company called eGroups. The company was eventually sold to Yahoo! in 2000 for $432 million in stock.

student. Carl Jr. also taught his younger brother how to take things apart and reassemble them. Larry practiced by taking apart many of the family's household mechanical devices and putting them back together, fostering a deep interest in learning how things worked. When Larry got to college, he put his mechanical skills to use creating an inkjet printer with Lego building blocks.

Larry was an excellent student and often impressed his teachers. He remembered being the first one in his elementary school to turn in a paper that was printed from a computer instead of handwritten. Carl Jr. realized Larry's aptitude, recalling, "One of the early things I remember Larry doing was typing [the book] *Frog and Toad Together* into his computer, one word at a time, when he was six years old."[2]

Larry's father instilled in his son a great talent for debate.

Sunrayce was a solar-powered car race for college students held every few years.

The two enjoyed lively arguments revolving around discussions of technology and going to rock concerts together.

COLLEGE DAYS

Larry graduated from East Lansing High School and enrolled in the computer-engineering program at the University of Michigan in Ann Arbor. Larry's extracurricular activities included membership in Eta Kappa Nu, the national honor society for electrical and computer engineering students.

Larry also became a member of the university's solar car team. The team built the 1993 Maize

LARRY'S INSPIRATION

At the age of 12, Larry read a biography of Nikola Tesla, a Serbian inventor considered the father of modern electrical engineering. Born in 1856, Tesla invented the alternating current (AC) electric power system and the radio. His ideas also laid the groundwork for remote control and radar. He immigrated to the United States at the age of 28 and became one of the greatest scientists and inventors of the late 1800s and early 1900s. Though his discoveries rivaled those of Thomas Edison—his former employer—Tesla struggled with finding practical applications for his inventions. And his eccentric behavior led many to view him as a mad scientist. Tesla died penniless and alone in a New York City hotel.

Larry was inspired by Tesla's work and viewed his life story as a cautionary example of not being able to apply an invention practically. Larry noted:

You don't want to be Tesla. He was one of the greatest inventors, but it's a sad, sad story. He couldn't commercialize anything, he could barely fund his own research. You'd want to be more like Edison. If you invent something, that doesn't necessarily help anybody. You've got to actually get it into the world; you've got to produce, make money doing it so you can fund it.[3]

& Blue, an early demonstration of an energy-efficient automobile. The vehicle took first place in the national Sunrayce 93 and eleventh place in the 1993 World Solar Challenge. Alternate power vehicles would interest Larry for years to come.

Larry graduated with honors from the University of Michigan with a bachelor's degree in engineering and a concentration in computer engineering. Although he had never lived outside Michigan, Larry decided to attend graduate school at Stanford University in California. Larry was a bit nervous heading that far from home, noting, "At first it was pretty scary. I kept complaining to my friends that I was going to get sent home on the bus. It didn't quite happen that way, however."[4]

A FORTUITOUS MEETING

In the spring of 1995, Larry headed to California to visit Stanford. His campus tour guide was Sergey Brin, a second-year student at the university. The two began to argue about various issues and continued debating over the course of two days. Each found the other opinionated, cocky, and obnoxious, as well as a formidable intellectual opponent.

Though Larry tended to be quiet and shy and Sergey was outgoing, they found an instant connection. As they argued, the two realized they shared many common interests, including an

"I just sort of kept having ideas. We had a lot of magazines lying around our house. It was kind of messy. So you kind of read stuff all the time, and I would read *Popular Science* and things like that. I just got interested in stuff, I guess, technology and how devices work. My brother taught me how to take things apart, and I took apart everything in the house. So I just became interested in it, for whatever reason, and so I had lots of ideas about what things could be built and how to build them and all these kinds of things. I built . . . an electric go-cart at a pretty early age."[5]

—*Larry Page*

obsession with computers and mathematics. They were also a bit wacky and loved to goof around. When Larry started classes in the fall, the two began hanging out together. The friendship would lead to a fortuitous partnership. +

Larry attended graduate school at Stanford University
in California, where he met Sergey.

Brin and Page's dorm room at Stanford might have
looked similar to this 2002 re-creation.

AN IDEA BECOMES REALITY

W hen Brin and Page met at Stanford, Brin
was in his second year at the university. He
had proven himself a math genius and had
aced the ten required exams for his doctoral program
on the first try. Many students make three attempts

before passing the exams. This meant Brin did not actually have to take any classes—he simply had to write a thesis in order to earn his PhD.

CAMPUS LIFE

Because his studies were so easy for him, Brin was able to devote time to his social life and other pursuits, including gymnastics, swimming, skiing, rollerblading, and even learning the trapeze. Brin's father once asked him if was taking any advanced courses, and his answer was, "Yes, advanced swimming."[1]

Since he tested out of his required classes, Brin had the opportunity to explore his own paths in computers, mathematics, and other academic subjects. He worked with students and professors on projects as varied as molecular biology, copyright violation detection programs, and a personalized movie rating system. One of his advisers noted, "He was a brash young man. But he was smart. It just oozed out of him."[2]

While the carefree Brin was enjoying his time at Stanford, Page was determined to invent something that would be useful and lucrative. Soon after arriving at Stanford, he set out to realize his dream.

He began studying Internet links and convinced Brin to join him. Both men realized the value of a better Internet search engine—one that would offer the user a ranking system based on importance rather than randomness.

BEG, BORROW, OR STEAL

Once the two men worked out the science behind the BackRub search engine and the PageRank algorithm, they had the groundwork for testing their theory that a search engine based on back links would prove more efficient for online searches. But they had one hurdle to overcome. They needed a lot of computers to store and process the vast amount of information on the Internet.

Page and Brin scavenged for any computers they could get their hands on. They occasionally visited the university's loading docks in search of equipment that had not yet been picked up by its owners. "We would just borrow a few machines, figuring if they didn't pick it up right away, they didn't need it so badly," Brin explained.[3]

As they gained processing power, the team was able to use a type of program called a spider to scour the Internet for Web sites. Next, they downloaded

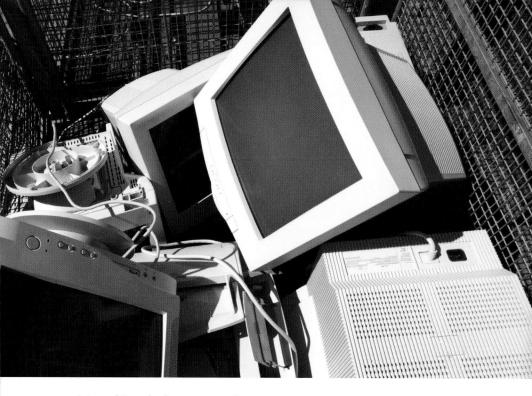

Brin and Page had to scrounge for computers to run their programs.

the Web sites onto their computers, where the sites could be analyzed for links. The process took longer than the two had first anticipated, and Page estimated that launching a spider cost the computer science department nearly $20,000.

But Page and Brin were enthusiastic about their project, and faculty members and fellow students began to show interest in and excitement for the new endeavor. Some of their advisers granted the two young men $10,000 to purchase equipment. They were also able to save money by constructing their own computers from used parts.

MAKING DO

Before long, their office was filled with computers. Lacking the physical space they needed to store the equipment, the team piled tall stacks of PCs in Page's dorm room. They discovered that their hodgepodge of misfit computers had an advantage. They were easy to repair and allowed the search engine to run faster. Brin and Page discovered that many smaller computers connected together worked better than one large one.

Page and Brin were almost inseparable. They spent most of their time together, usually in their office, excitedly

WEB CRAWLERS

Internet search engines work through the use of specialized software that sends out a spider. The spider, or Web crawler, is a computer program that checks Web sites, retrieving data that it brings back to the computer's database. The data is fed into an indexer, which analyzes it based on programmed criteria and builds an index of Web sites. Typically, Web crawlers are scouting constantly to update their index. When a user types in a search term, the search engine uses the index to create a result list containing Web pages and their URLs.

The problem with this method was it did not provide a results list based on usefulness or importance for the user. BackRub, however, utilized PageRank to bring order to searches. The algorithm, which included more than 500 million variables and 2 billion terms, allowed the search engine to assign value and rank Web pages according to the back links. The calculations performed by the algorithm during the search are performed in a fraction of a second, providing the user with a results list in about a half a second. This method of search was the first of its kind.

discussing BackRub or bantering back and forth about other topics. Other students started referring to the pair as one unit—LarryandSergey.

THE ADVENT OF GOOGLE

By the fall of 1997, the two decided they needed a catchier name for their BackRub search engine. Brin and Page began brainstorming. It seemed that every idea they came up with had already been used. They turned to office mate Sean Anderson for help. After days of failing to settle on a new name, frustration set in. Anderson remembered:

> *[Page] started getting desperate, and we had another brain-storming session. I was sitting at the whiteboard and one of the last things I came up with was, "How about Googleplex? You are trying to come up with a company that searches and indexes and allows people to*

THE GATES 360 CREW

In January 1996, Stanford's Computer Science Department moved into a new building on campus: William Gates Computer Science Building. There, Brin and Page shared office number 360 with four other graduate students. The students were brilliant and quirky. Lucas Periera was a bundle of energy, and Tamara Munzner described herself as a complete geek. Ben Zhu barely spoke to the others. Sean Anderson filled the crowded space with plants and a self-watering system he created, and he eventually started living and sleeping in the office. Despite their peculiarities, they all got along well.

organize vast amounts of data. Googleplex is a huge number." He liked that.[4]

Page liked the idea for the new name and suggested they shorten it to Google. The word *googol* is the number 1 followed by 100 zeroes. Anderson explained:

I typed in G-o-o-g-l-e and misspelled it on my workstation, and that was available. Larry found that acceptable, and he registered it later that evening and wrote it on the whiteboard: Google.com. It had a wild Internet ring to it, like Yahoo or Amazon.[5]

The next morning, one of their office mates pointed out that they had misspelled *googol*. Misspelled or not, Google had been born.

GOOGOL

The word *googol* was coined by nine-year-old Milton Sirotta in 1938. Milton's uncle, Edward Kasner, was a US mathematician who used the term in *Mathematics and the Imagination*, a book he cowrote with James Newman that was published in 1940.

SUCCESS AT STANFORD

Brin and Page enlisted the help of faculty adviser Rajeev Motwani in preparing the search engine as a prototype for internal use at Stanford. Faculty and students were able to use Google, which was then online at google.standford.edu. Users provided Brin and Page with feedback about how well they felt the search engine worked. Users were excited to finally have a search engine that produced results ranked by their value.

The university helped Brin and Page seek a patent for their creation. The young men set out to redesign the home page. For BackRub, Page had simply photocopied his hand and used the image as his logo. The team did not have money to hire a designer, so Brin and Page did it themselves. They opted for a plain white background with primary colors for the word Google. Its simple, uncluttered look, free of flashy ads and busy graphics, was attractive to users.

The search engine proved to be a much better tool than its counterparts at the time. Brin and Page were confident in their program. They had outgrown their office and dorm

PAGERANK PATENTED

On January 9, 1998, Stanford University filed a patent application for the PageRank process. US Patent 6,285,999 was issued September 4, 2001. It listed Stanford University as the holder of the patent, giving the institution the rights to it—anyone else who wanted to use the algorithm would have to obtain permission. Larry Page was designated as the inventor. Stanford still holds the rights to PageRank. In exchange for use of the patent, Google gave Stanford 1.8 million stock shares, which it sold in 2005 for $336 million.

"Not since Gutenberg invented the modern printing press more than 500 years ago, making books and scientific tomes affordable and widely available to the masses, has any new invention empowered individuals, and transformed access to information, as profoundly as Google."[6]

—David A. Vise,
The Google Story

room computer centers, and the Stanford administration was growing frustrated with the bandwidth Google was using on the university's server. Brin and Page were ready to sell Google to a company or an investor. They hoped they would be able to turn a tidy profit for their creation and then continue graduate school. But things did not quite turn out that way. +

Brin and Page created the Google logo with
simple lettering and bold colors.

Brin and Page wanted to sell Google to the search
engine company AltaVista.

BUSINESS VENTURE

From the beginning, neither Brin nor Page intended to make Google into a business. They both viewed it as a scholarly research project that would propel them closer to their PhD degrees. Instead of becoming professors as their fathers had, however, the two men followed in the footsteps of many other inventive Stanford students.

The hype surrounding Google continued to grow at Stanford. Brin and Page were well on their way to becoming another powerhouse in Silicon Valley. But first, they had to find a way to expand Google beyond Stanford. Brin and Page believed if they sold Google to a preexisting search engine that could use the technology to improve searching, they would make a nice profit and then continue with their studies.

NO LUCK SELLING

In 1997, Brin and Page contacted one of the creators of AltaVista, which was then considered the best Internet search engine. They hoped AltaVista would be interested in purchasing Google for $1 million. Paul Flaherty, a Stanford graduate and AltaVista executive, listened to Brin and Page describe Google's superiority. "I felt they really had something with their link-based approach to page ranking, which was AltaVista's technical weakness at the time," he said.[1] But in the end, AltaVista's parent company, Digital Equipment Corp. (DEC), decided against the purchase.

Brin and Page pitched their creation to Excite and Yahoo! as well, but neither was interested. But their meeting with Yahoo! cofounder David Filo was not completely fruitless. Filo suggested that if they believed they had a special product with Google, they should consider taking a break from their studies and launching the business themselves.

They decided not to make any major decisions and focused on improving Google for its users at Stanford. They sent out e-mail surveys asking users for feedback. The results prompted the duo to add a small summary for each search result, improving Google's usability and creating more loyal users.

SILICON VALLEY

Stanford University is located in the middle of Silicon Valley, the area south of the San Francisco Bay area. In the 1940s and 1950s, Stanford's dean of engineering, Frederick Terman, encouraged Stanford graduates to remain in the area and start companies. He convinced the university to develop hundreds of acres of land to build offices and research facilities, known as an industrial park. Stanford Research Park was established, and it nurtured high-tech firms such as Hewlett-Packard, one of the world's largest computer technology companies. Aided by some of the most brilliant minds in the industry, powerful companies in the fields of radio, television, military electronics, and computers evolved there.

By the 1970s, the area was blooming with semiconductor and computer companies. Silicon is an essential ingredient in semiconductors. So many companies dealing with semiconductors sprang up around Stanford University that the region became known as Silicon Valley.

Daily searches reached more than 10,000. As demand for Google grew, the team needed more processing power and more memory. They continued to acquire computers when they could and eventually reached the limits of three credit cards buying disk space. They were running out of hope that someone would want to buy Google. Brin and Page began to realize they would probably have to start their own business if they wanted Google to expand.

AN ANGEL INVESTOR

Starting a business requires large amounts of money. Wealthy individuals who invest their own money in a start-up company are called angel investors. In exchange for start-up funds, they are usually granted an ownership portion in the company. If the start-up does well, these investors often make a lot of money.

Brin and Page turned to computer science professor David Cheriton for help finding investors. In August 1998, Cheriton introduced the men to Andy Bechtolsheim, a Silicon Valley entrepreneur. Bechtolsheim was the vice president of Cisco Systems, a technology company. He was interested in what the students described to him. Bechtolsheim liked that Google solved a simple problem of finding information, and he admired the intellect and drive of the two young inventors. After briefly discussing how Google could be profitable, Bechtolsheim wrote out a check on the spot to Google Inc. for $100,000. Brin and Page would not be able to cash the check until they officially started their company. Cheriton agreed to match the investment.

EARLY BEGINNINGS IN A GARAGE

Google was underway. Brin and Page had the funding they needed, and on September 7, 1998, Google officially became a corporation. The paperwork listed Page as the chief executive officer (CEO) and Brin as president. Their mission statement read simply, "To make it easier to find high-quality information on the Web."[2]

The two put their scholarly pursuits on hold. Their parents were not pleased. Brin's mother recalled, "We were definitely upset.

A SAD DEPARTURE

Adviser Terry Winograd recalled when Brin and Page left school to pursue Google. "I remember the day they cleaned out their offices," he said, "I remember that day because they were very disappointed. They had this grim look on their face[s] because they had to go to Stanford with empty boxes, and leave with them full."[3]

Google's first company headquarters was in this garage in Menlo Park, California.

We thought everybody in their right mind ought to get a PhD."[4]

No longer students, they had to leave Stanford. They needed new headquarters and a place to live. They rented a spare bedroom and a garage from Brin's girlfriend's sister, Susan Wojcicki. Since home and work were now under the same roof, Brin and Page were nearly always together in one place. Google's office was affordable and functional.

But within a few months, Brin and Page would outgrow the garage space they rented for their company.

LANDLADY, EMPLOYEE, AND FUTURE SISTER-IN-LAW

The owner of Brin and Page's garage, Susan Wojcicki, provided them with more than space in her home. In 1999, she was put to work as Google's first marketing professional. Her early duties included creating holiday logos for Google and managing licensing for Web search with the corporation's first customers. She eventually became vice president of product management. Her husband, Dennis Troper, also serves as an operational executive. In 2007, Susan Wojcicki became Sergey Brin's sister-in-law when he married her sister, Anne.

THE GROWTH OF GOOGLE

By the end of 1998, Google was featured in *USA Today*. Although the company was new, *PC Magazine* listed it in its Top 100 Web Sites and Search Engines for 1998, saying Google "has an uncanny knack for returning extremely relevant results."[5] People were beginning to take note of Google and its novel approach to Internet searching.

Google was gaining exposure and growing quickly. The Google guys decided it was time to expand. Shortly after securing the investment money from Bechtolsheim, Brin and Page hired Craig Silverstein, a fellow Stanford PhD student, as Google's first employee. After five months of working out of the garage, the men rented office space in downtown Palo Alto, only one mile (1.6 km) from Stanford.

Brin and Page began hiring more brilliant young graduates and realized they would have to expand again soon. In June 1999, the company received $25 million from two investment companies. With the investment money backing them, they were able to move the company's headquarters to a larger office in Mountain View, California, in August.

Although the men no longer had to scrounge for funding or equipment, they still committed themselves to developing their corporation as frugally as possible. They opted for cheaper computers rather than high-end models. And, they stripped the machines of unnecessary parts that slowed processing time.

WHERE IT ALL BEGAN

In 2006, to celebrate the company's eighth birthday, Google purchased Susan Wojcicki's home, where Google began as a garage start-up. They bought the house for an estimated $1 million. The home has become a tourist attraction, with busloads of people stopping to take pictures of Google's historic landmark.

"It kind of seems surprising in retrospect, but at the time it was a bunch of little steps and they all made a lot of sense. That algorithm turned into a really successful search engine at Stanford. A bunch of Stanford people used it. I saw it at that point and was really enamored of it. . . . I was really impressed to see something that was so much better than the state of the art. So it became a company, it started growing users by word of mouth, and now we're like this."[6]

—Craig Silverstein, Google's first employee

UNLIKE OTHER SEARCH ENGINES

Perhaps one of the most important keys to the success of Google was that other commercial search engines were not interested in creating a better search tool. High-profile search engines such as AltaVista, Excite, and Lycos were owned by companies that made money through other avenues, such as advertising. As search quality deteriorated on these sites, users looked for alternatives. They found Google.

Other search engine companies were convinced a savvy search engine was not important, but Brin and Page held fast to their firm belief that a fast, reliable, and accurate search engine would prove its worth in the long run. The men put their money into additional servers and allowed word of mouth and favorable media coverage to do their marketing for them. The results were faster Google searches and happier users who shared the news of Google with others. The base of the site's users continued to grow even as the company spent no money on marketing.

AGAINST ADVERTISING

Other search engines were willing to sell ad banners on their Web sites, but Brin and Page were adamantly against it. They were proud of their clean, uncluttered home page and did not want to compromise the site's purpose: to search, not to sell. While at Stanford, the men had written a paper, "The Anatomy of a Large-Scale Hypertextual Web Search Engine," in which they described their PageRank algorithm and their plans for turning it into a cutting-edge search engine. In it, they explained, "Advertising-funded search engines will inherently be biased toward the advertisers and away from the needs of the consumers."[7]

By the end of 1999, Google searches had increased to an average of 7 million per day. Within six months, that number swelled to 18 million. The press continued to praise Google, and the buzz continued to grow. The company was spending more than $500,000 a month in operating costs, and that figure was climbing as Google continued to expand to meet user needs. Google allowed other companies to use its search technology for a fee, but, even with this income, it would soon run out of money. It looked as though Brin and Page would need to change their minds about selling advertising. +

icrosoft Corporation - Windows Internet Explorer

M http://www.microsoft.com/en/us/default.aspx

| Edit | View | Favorites | Tools | Help |

M Microsoft Corporation

Microsoft

e Yahoo! - Windows Inte

Y! http://m

| File | Edit | View | Favori |

Y! Yahoo!

YAHC

My Yahoo!   Make Y! you

MY FAVORITES

View Yahoo! Site

Yahoo! Mail

Autos

eBay

pping   Gmail   more ▼

Google™

Google Search   I'm Feeling Lucky

Google's uncluttered home page made it different from
other search engines, including Yahoo!.

Google began including ads with its search results
called "Sponsored Links."

MAKING A PROFIT

With millions of daily Google searches but very slim profits, Brin and Page reluctantly agreed to begin allowing advertising on their Web site. It was the only way they saw to become a profitable company. Clearly, users were not about to start paying for Google service. But as was their custom from the start, the partners wanted to do it their way. They had adopted the motto Don't Be Evil, meaning that they wanted to do what they felt was best for Google users instead of allowing profit to guide their actions. Brin and Page had to figure out a way to go forward with advertising sales without compromising Google's mantra.

DOING IT THEIR WAY

Google users had come to expect the clean look of the Google Web page. When Marissa Mayer, their second employee, had changed the Google results font for easier reading in December 1999, she experienced an outcry from users. With this previous experience, Brin and Page were not eager to change the overall look of their home page to include advertising—it would be a delicate matter.

By May 2000, Google's Internet searches topped 18 million searches a day, and in June, Google

"DON'T BE EVIL"

In July 2001, Google's employees met to come up with some core principles they believed represented Google. Some offered mottos such as "Treat Everyone with Respect" and "Be on Time for Meetings." Paul Buchheit, a Google engineer, blurted out, "All of these things can be covered by just saying, 'Don't Be Evil.'"[1] The phrase stuck and has become part of Google's culture.

OFFENSIVE SEARCH RESULTS

The founders of Google insist that Internet search results lists remain free and available to anyone looking to search. However, observers have also argued that certain information should not be available to everyone on the Web, such as instructions on how to make a bomb.

Brin and Page, both of Jewish descent, were forced to question their policy of uncensored search results when it was discovered that conducting a search with the word Jew returned an anti-Semitic Web site called Jew-Watch toward the top of the results list.

Jewish groups demanded the Web site be removed from the top of Google's listings. Brin, who had moved from Russia with his family as a child to escape anti-Semitism, refused to remove the site. He explained, "I certainly am very offended by the site, but the objectivity of our rankings is one of our very important principles."[2]

Instead, Google compromised by displaying an "Offensive Search Results" warning at the top of search results pages with questionable Web sites. The warning is a link that brings the user to an explanation of Google's policy on questionable results. "Our search results are generated completely objectively and are independent of the beliefs and preferences of those who work at Google."[3]

announced its index had reached 1 billion URLs, making it the top Internet search engine. Google had gathered an enormous audience for potential advertisers. With US companies spending billions of dollars annually for advertising on radios, billboards, buses, and in print, Google could offer them a new venue for reaching consumers.

Through Google, advertisers could target consumers who were specifically looking for the product advertisers were selling. For example, placing an advertisement for a camera on a billboard did not promise that people driving by would be interested in purchasing a camera. However, if a person searched Google for information about cameras, that person was more likely to be thinking about buying a camera at the time. There was no better time to place an advertisement for a camera, or camera equipment, right in front of the user.

Brin and Page agreed they would not clutter their clean home page with ads. Instead, they would permit advertising on the results page. Advertisements would display at the top of the results list in a light blue box, separating them from the pure white background. This allowed them to offer a free, unbiased results list the user could differentiate from paid advertisements. If the user wanted to know more, they could click on an ad's link. Additionally, Google titled these "Sponsored Links," feeling it would lend more credibility to the ads.

The team was able to keep its search engine running smoothly, free of annoying pop-ups and graphics. All Google ads looked the same: a headline, a link, and a short description of the Web site. Advertisers were able to purchase Google advertising space online. They bid on keywords, which triggered their ads to appear above the results list when a user

ADSENSE

In 2003, Google developed AdSense, which allows Web sites to display AdWords advertisements on their own sites. Web site owners make money when a visitor clicks on the advertisement, and the advertiser is charged. Soon, however, click fraud began to occur. This happens when a person or an automated program clicks on the ad just to make more money for the Web site owner. Google continues to improve at identifying fraudulent clicks, but sometimes it is difficult to judge whether a click is legitimate. Industry estimates of the rate of click fraud vary widely from 2 percent to 20 percent of all clicks.

performed a search. The company that paid the most for a keyword had top billing in the Sponsored Links box.

The men behind the brilliant PageRank system saw an opportunity to apply the same logic to advertising. Brin and Page explained, "We look at ads as commercial information, and that goes back to our core mission of organizing the world's information."[4] They soon developed AdWords, a system by which advertisements gain a quality score based on how many users click them. The assumption was that advertisements with more clicks were valued more by Web users, just as Web pages had been ranked by PageRank. The quality scores of these ads could grow until they showed up higher in the search results than the advertisements with the highest keyword bid. Once again, Brin and Page were placing the power in the hands of the users.

The Google guys had a profitable business approach and a staff of more than 150 by the end of 2000. They allowed other search sites, such as Yahoo! and America Online (AOL), to use Google technology for a fee. Their sale of advertising space decreased the need to use investment money for operating costs, and by 2001, their daily searches hit 100 million, or 1,000 every second. The word *google* had even become part of everyday speech for many English speakers.

But Google had yet to turn a profit, and the duo was being pressured by the company's investors to bring in a new CEO with business expertise to help make money from Google's popularity and success.

A NEW CEO

In August 2001, Eric Schmidt was hired as Google's new CEO. Brin became president of technology at the company, while Page was put in charge of

SOME CENSORSHIP FOR THE GOOGLE GUYS

While Brin and Page have been diligent not to restrict search result lists in the name of freedom of information, there was one aspect of Google they did not mind censoring. They decided to not allow AdWords ads to be sold for cigarettes, tobacco, or guns.

\GŪ-GƏL\

On June 15, 2006, the *Oxford English Dictionary* added *google* as a verb, meaning, "To use the Google search engine to find information on the Internet. To search for information about (a person or thing) using the Google search engine."[6] The following year, the American Dialect Society chose the word as the "most useful" word of 2002.[7]

products. The three would share power and decision making in the company. Schmidt had been chief technology officer at Sun Microsystems and CEO of Novell, two successful technology companies. Brin and Page were impressed with his business skills and his demeanor, and the investors were relieved to have an experienced—and successful—Silicon Valley executive running things. Schmidt noticed that the young men, both still under the age of 30, were talented. He said:

[They] had remarkably good judgment for such young people. It's intelligence, but also street smarts, insight. It's very impressive. It took me twenty years to develop the insights they had learned in two or three.[5]

Within one month of becoming CEO, Schmidt helped Google make a profit for the first time. By the end of the year, Google's 2001 revenues approached nearly $85 million. The graduate students' school project had become a profitable business. +

Eric Schmidt, *top*, became Google's new CEO in 2001.

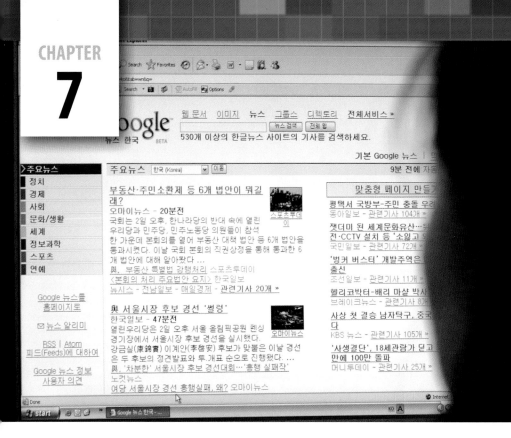

A user reading Google search results in Korean in 2006

GOOGLE GROWS UP

Brin and Page continued to improve their search engine. In May 2000, Google came out with search abilities in ten additional languages: French, German, Italian, Swedish, Finnish, Spanish, Portuguese, Dutch, Norwegian, and Danish. Within four months, they added Chinese, Japanese, and Korean. By 2002, they served 72 languages. People worldwide were googling.

Developers at Google were hard at work, and by July 2001, Google users could explore more than 250 million images with the Google Images search. The following month, Brin and Page found themselves in Tokyo, Japan, for the opening of their first international office.

Brin and Page signed a landmark deal with AOL in May 2002. AOL would use Google's search technology and paid ad listings to reach its 34 million customers. The deal made Google a major player on the Internet, alongside Internet powerhouses such as Yahoo!, Amazon, and eBay.

LIFE AT THE GOOGLEPLEX

In March 2004, the company moved into an even bigger headquarters building, staying in

WHIMSICAL GOOGLE

The corporate climate at Google has always made room for fun-loving wit and whimsy. Each April 1, April Fools' Day, the Google home page makes funny, fake claims. In the past, the company has claimed its searches were powered by pigeons and changed its name from Google to Topeka. In the same vein, among the 130 languages now supported by Google are Pig Latin, Elmer Fudd, Bork, Bork, Bork! (spoken by the Muppets' Swedish Chef), and Star Trek's Klingon.

GOOGLEPLEX

Google's headquarters in Mountain View, California, is called the Googleplex. The name is a combination of the words *google* and *complex*, but there is also a mathematical definition. The word *googolplex* refers to the number 10 to the power of googol (1 followed by 100 zeroes).

Mountain View. The new corporate campus came to be known as the Googleplex. Workers at the Googleplex enjoyed a laid-back, fun atmosphere that countered the stress of some of their projects. The company offered everything from massages to pool tables and free laundry to free food. The hype surrounding Google allowed Brin and Page to hire enthusiastic employees who were eager to be part of a cutting-edge corporation. The perks were an attractive bonus, but people were expected to perform at Google. One employee noted:

> *Twelve hours a day, six days a week was typical. It was optional, but there was pressure to do it. They fed you all the time, so there was no reason to leave for food. Google was a twenty-four/seven lifestyle. And they were all such nice people.* [1]

Google employees work in a fun office environment.

In addition, Brin and Page allowed software engineers to spend 20 percent of their time working on projects that interested them. They felt this would spark more innovation and creativity. Krishna Bharat, a Google engineer, explained:

The 20 percent time was invented for people to just explore. People are productive when they are

A DAY IN THE LIFE

In order to inspire the brilliant minds working for them, Brin and Page fostered creativity at the Googleplex. The entrepreneurs wanted employees to be excited about coming to work. The Google work culture has been described as "part university campus and part kindergarten playground."[3]

Instead of walled offices and cubicles, employees shared an open office space. Lava lamps, pool tables, and foosball games gave the office a casual, entertaining atmosphere to make their jobs less stressful. Employees were free to take advantage of napping areas, yoga classes, and an on-site masseuse.

And staff did not have to go far to find something to eat. A chef cooked free gourmet meals for the employees, and refrigerators and snack bars were filled with free, healthful food options. Pets were even allowed in the office, and the dress code simply stated employees had to wear "something"—which sometimes translated into pajamas, a bathrobe, and slippers. Googlers, as employees came to be called, worked in a comfortable environment, free of the stuffy rules of the typical corporate world. The perks expanded to include bicycles employees use to ride from building to building, free laundry rooms, and Segway scooters.

working on things they see as important or they have invented, or are working on something they are passionate about.[2]

Although salaries were relatively low, employees rarely talked about money. Most were there because they were excited to be part of Google. Plus, most knew enough about successful start-ups in Silicon Valley to know that once the company started selling stock shares to the public, the employees would make a lot of money.

AUGUST 19, 2004

On August 19, 2004, Google offered stock

shares for public purchase for the first time. This is called an initial public offering, or IPO. Page was in New York City at the stock exchange when trading began, while Brin stayed at the Googleplex with the company's employees. Google's entire team was eager to see if the company's stock would sell—and for how much.

As trading commenced, Google stock was offered at $85 per share. By the end of the day, more than 19 million shares had been sold, and the price had risen to almost $100. The following day, shares reached $108.31 and kept climbing. Within three months, Google stock topped $200 per share. By the summer of 2005, the price per share held at around $300. By October 2007, stock prices increased to more than $600 per share, rising above stock prices of rival computer technology powerhouses Microsoft and Yahoo!, as well as large companies including Walmart and Coca-Cola. Those holding shares purchased for $85 each were rewarded with a more than 600 percent increase on their initial purchase price.

Brin and Page became billionaires and raised more than $3 billion in cash for the company. The men were ranked at 43 on the Forbes 400 list of the wealthiest Americans in 2004, each worth

$4 billion. The young men who had put their educations on hold had become two of the wealthiest individuals in the United States. And Google was still growing. +

Google's stock exchange price kept climbing after the company
started selling stock shares to the public.

Google expanded into larger headquarters in Palo Alto, California, in 2004.

EXPANSION AND OPPOSITION

I n 2004, Brin and Page, now 31-year-old billionaires, were still living modest lifestyles. Neither man particularly liked being in the spotlight. In an interview after the stock sale, Page was asked if he had gotten used to the fame. He said:

I'm not really used to it. I just want to invent things and get them out into the world. I feel really lucky that I have the ability to affect things now. It's a tremendous responsibility to use that for good. . . . I feel more pressure to do things that matter. I'm responsible to a lot of people now.[1]

GOOGLE: BIGGER AND BETTER

Brin and Page were being recognized for Google's impact on the world. They continued opening offices around the globe, including locations in Ireland, India, and Australia. In addition to global expansion, Google was launching exciting and innovative technology.

In December 2003, Google launched the first version of Google Book Search, which allowed online users to see excerpts of scanned versions of books. Within a year, Google

BOOKS IN ENGLISH

When Google announced Google Book Search in 2004, the president of France's national library at the time, Jean-Noël Jeanneney, expressed concern the project might damage the world's cultural heritage. Jeanneney subsequently wrote about this concern in *Google and the Myth of Universal Knowledge: A View from Europe.* "We must wonder what books will be chosen, what criteria will determine the list." Noting most books would be English or English translations, he warned, "What is at stake is language, of course, and we can see how the use of English (in its American form) threatens to become ever more prevalent at the expense of other European languages."[2]

YOUTUBE

YouTube was designed by three men who wanted a Web site where users, including themselves, could share videos easily. YouTube's beta site went online in early 2005. The Web site officially launched late that year and quickly became the Internet's largest video sharing site. The free online service has become home to more than 100 million amateur and professional videos, including home movies, television clips, movie trailers, music videos, and video blog entries.

YouTube's first video was uploaded on April 23, 2005, and featured one of the creators at a zoo. Google purchased YouTube for $1.65 billion in 2006.

was collaborating with the libraries of Harvard University, Stanford University, the University of Michigan, Oxford University, and the New York Public Library. They scanned books that were no longer restricted by copyright and offered them to users in what became Google Library.

In spring 2004, Brin and Page announced Gmail, Google's version of e-mail. Gmail offered users 500 times greater storage space than Microsoft e-mail and 250 times more than Yahoo!, all for free.

In February 2005, Google Images hit a landmark: 1.1 billion indexed images. That same month, Google Maps launched, offering Google users an alternative to MapQuest for digital maps and driving directions. Later that year, Google Earth went online, creating a model of Earth that allowed users to zoom in from space to see any part of the globe in 3-D.

t View Favorites Tools Help

Forward | Stop | Refresh | Home | Search | Media | Favorites | History | Print | Copy | Cut | Paste

http://gmail.google.com/gmail

Mail
BETA

| Contacts | Settings | Help

[Search Mail] [Search the Web]

Show search options Create a filter

se Mail

« Back to Inbox | Archive | Report Spam | More actions... ▾

‹ Newe

Gmail is different. Here's what you need to know. Inbox [Apply label... ▾]

☆ Gmail Team <gmail-noreply@google.com> to me   More options Apr 9

First off, welcome. And thanks for agreeing to help us test Gmail. By now you probably know the key ways in which Gmail differs from traditional webmail services. Searching instead of filing. A free gigabyte of storage. Messages displayed in context as conversations.

So what else is new?

Gmail has many other special features that will become apparent as you use your account. You'll find answers to most of your questions in our searchable help section, which includes a Getting Started guide. You'll find information there on such topics as:

- How to use address auto-complete
- Setting up filters for incoming mail
- Using advanced search options

You may also have noticed some text ads or related links to the right of this message. They're placed there in the same way that ads are placed alongside Google search results and, through our AdSense program, on content pages across the web. The matching of ads to content in your Gmail messages is performed entirely by computers; never by people. Because the ads and links are matched to information that is of interest to you, we hope you'll find them relevant and useful.

You're one of the very first people to use Gmail. Your input will help determine how it evolves, so we encourage you to send your feedback, suggestions and questions to us. But mostly, we hope you'll enjoy experimenting with Google's approach to email.

Speedy Delivery,

The Gmail Team

Open in new
Print convers
Expand all

Sponsored Li
AdSense Tracker
Detailed tracking incl
clicks and CTR for e
of your site
markcarey.com/AdS
Doing AdWords Y
Definitive guide to 2
PPC tactics & free p
newsletter.
www.Page-Zero.co
Affiliate makes $4
How does Mike ban
monthly? He market:
tiny ad. aff
www.compare-fun
$4680

Related Pag
The page cannot be
The page you are lo
might have been ren
had its ...
www.thisdayonline
Searching With Ope
Opera has a built in
function that lets yo
the Web ...
www.opera.com
Search DiVued Boo

Early testers of Gmail received messages similar to this one.

In October 2006, Google purchased the online video entertainment community YouTube for $1.65 billion. The acquisition merged two of the most recognized online companies. In a press statement, Google promised:

> [The new team will] focus on providing a better, more comprehensive experience for users interested in uploading, watching, and sharing

GOOGLE MAPS AND STREET VIEW

In May 2007, Google launched Street View for Google Maps. Street View gave users a panoramic view of the street location they mapped on Google Maps. Users were able to travel along streets while zooming in and out for better views of the area, giving them a better sense of the location than a map alone.

Cars equipped with cameras captured images in a 360-degree range. Google used snowmobiles and a custom pedal tricycle to capture images in areas cars could not travel, such as narrow alleyways and ski slopes.

In its beginning stages, only large US metropolitan areas had Street View. By 2010, the feature offered views in all 50 states and several European countries, including France, Italy, Germany, the United Kingdom, and the Czech Republic. Japan, South Africa, and Australia had recently become available, with new areas being added all the time.

Privacy advocates have criticized the service. In many areas, private homes are clearly visible. In some instances, the zoom feature allows users to see inside people's homes. In other still images, car license plates are clearly visible. Many argue Street View is an invasion of privacy and poses a security threat.

videos, and will offer new opportunities for professional content owners to distribute their work to reach a vast new audience.[3]

But as Google continued to come out with cutting-edge technology, not everyone was on the Google bandwagon.

LAWSUITS

American Blinds, a US company that sells window blinds, wallpaper, and other interior decorating products, purchased AdWords for the search term *blinds*, as well as the company name. The company soon discovered competitors were able to outbid them for the words *American blinds.* Customers who searched for that term would be brought to competitors' Web sites.

A similar situation arose with large US automobile insurer Geico. Both companies sued Google in 2004, filing lawsuits for trademark infringement. In the end, both lawsuits were dismissed. However, Google lost similar cases in Europe.

THE QUESTION OF PRIVACY

Gmail has also come under fire by privacy advocates. The new e-mail system was making money by placing ads next to e-mail messages. Google computers scanned e-mails and placed ads with them based on the contents of the messages. It did not take long for privacy advocates and politicians to attack Google's new attempt at making profits. The *Wall Street Journal*'s technology columnist, Walt Mossberg, reported:

> *The problem here isn't confusion between ads and editorial content. It's that Google is scanning your private email to locate the keywords that generate the ads. This seems like an invasion of privacy.*[4]

In addition to the outcry about e-mail scanning, privacy advocates noted that Google had the ability to catalog the Internet searches users were conducting. There was a growing concern that Google could turn this information over to authorities.

Brin and Page were surprised by the opposition to Gmail. In the end, they pointed out that their privacy practices were similar to those of other e-mail services, and they agreed to destroy closed accounts or deleted e-mails as quickly as possible.

THE BATTLE IN CHINA

As Google has grown and developed, so has its impact on the world. With offices in 36 countries and 20 in the United States alone, Google has become an international success. But not every location has agreed with the search engine's policies.

THE CHINA DILEMMA

Brin and Page were criticized for allowing Google's China site to be censored. Shareholders at annual meetings protested that Google should pull out of China for human rights reasons. Brin was defensive about their decision, knowing other search engines had been forced to do the same thing. When forced to defend the decision at a shareholder meeting, Brin asked one protestor which search engine he would switch to. When the man named Yahoo!, Brin replied, "Oh, you mean the company that just turned over information about one of its users to the Chinese government and got him arrested?"[5]

In January 2006, Google China—Google.cn—debuted. In a controversial decision, Google chose to comply with Internet censorship laws in the country, which does not allow the same freedoms of speech as the United States. Rather than receiving a results list, users searching prohibited words were directed to a page explaining their search results did not comply with current laws and regulations.

Brin and Page were criticized for allowing Google to censor search results in China. Many critics argued this practice was in violation of their own motto, Don't Be Evil. Many believed Google should not block a population of more than 1 billion people from receiving complete information. But the partners faced a difficult dilemma—if they did not comply with Chinese law, the company might be barred from the country.

CROSS-CULTURAL CENSORSHIP

From culture to culture, what is deemed appropriate for censorship varies. Child pornography is deemed inappropriate nearly worldwide. Some countries censor other types of violent or sexual content. Some US laws require schools and libraries to block certain content from children.

In the United States, freedom of speech allows people to create and access all but the most objectionable content. Other countries have different laws. For example, Germany blocks some racist content that would be allowed under US laws. Iran heavily censors the Internet, blocking sites considered disrespectful to the country's religion, Islam. Many countries, including Iran and China, block Internet communications that speak against their governments.

In January 2010, Google announced it would no longer censor search results in China. Throughout the spring, Google automatically redirected users in China through its Hong Kong site, which was not censored. The Chinese government threatened to ban Google from China. In June, the company compromised by placing a link to Google Hong Kong on the Google China Web site but not automatically redirecting users there. China accepted the compromise, but the root causes of the problem remained unresolved. As long as China wished to censor Internet results and Google remained against censorship, tensions between the company and the country would continue. +

Google

谷歌

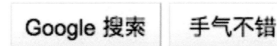

| Google 搜索 | 手气不错 |

google.com.hk

请收藏我们的网址

音乐   翻译   购物

© 2010 · ICP证合字B2-20070004号

Beginning in June 2010, the Google China home page had a link to
the Hong Kong site to allow users to avoid censorship.

Page shakes hands with Bill Clinton, *right*, at an event for the former
president's charitable organization, the Clinton Global Initiative.

THE BILLIONAIRE
PHILANTHROPISTS

E ach year, Google continued to add to Brin's
and Page's wealth. Each man's stock shares were
worth billions of dollars. Even so, Brin's mother
still hoped her son would return to Stanford to finish
his PhD. The Google duo was making huge amounts

of money each month through the sale of stock shares—sometimes as much as $70 million—and agreed to draw a yearly salary of only $1. CEO Eric Schmidt was in the same position and agreed to the same salary.

Employees and investors were also cashing in portions of their stock and making millions. Some purchased new homes for millions of dollars, while others showed up at work in lavish sports cars. The long hours and modest salaries Googlers had endured were paying off handsomely. Google was a company of millionaires. Even the executive chef and on-site masseuse made millions.

MINIMUM WAGES

Brin and Page were not the first business leaders to opt out of drawing large salaries. Steve Jobs, founder of Apple Computers, began taking a $1 yearly salary in 1998. Cisco Systems CEO John Chambers reduced his salary from $350,000 to $1 in 2001 when his company experienced poor economic performance. But as soon as Cisco began to recover financially, his full salary was reinstated.

GOOGLE.ORG: SHARING THE WEALTH

Brin and Page began plans for a philanthropic organization in 2004, when Google went public and offered its stock. This was the beginning of Google.org. Page had ambitious dreams for

THE MASSEUSE RETIRES

Bonnie Brown, Google's first masseuse, spent five years massaging the backs of Google's hardworking engineers and programmers. Her part-time position began with a weekly salary of $450. She also received stock options. When she cashed them in, Brown received millions of dollars. She is now retired and receives weekly massages herself. She wrote a book about her good fortune titled *Giigle: How I Got Lucky Massaging Google.*

Google.org, "We hope someday [Google.org] may eclipse Google itself in terms of overall world impact by ambitiously applying innovation and significant resources to the largest of the world's problems."[1]

The men pledged 1 percent of Google's profits and 1 percent of employee time to build "technology products to address global challenges such as climate change, pandemic disease, and poverty."[2] Brin and Page added other philanthropic programs to their corporation. Google also offers resources for promoting reading, conducts technology workshops for children, and gives scholarships annually to outstanding undergraduate and graduate female computer science students.

WEDDING BELLS

Throughout their rise from Stanford graduate students to billionaires, Brin and Page worked

Brin and his wife, Anne, live in a quiet neighborhood in Palo Alto.

hard to keep their personal lives as private as possible. Neither was interested, or comfortable, in the spotlight of fame. Nevertheless, it was difficult for men of such wealth and influence to live completely anonymous lives. When each man married, tabloids were abuzz with rumors of the upcoming weddings.

Brin's mother had always hoped her son would marry "somebody exciting who could be really interesting to him."[3] In May 2007, she got her wish when Brin married Anne Wojcicki, sister of Brin and Page's garage landlady, Susan Wojcicki. The wedding's location was kept strictly confidential—guests were told simply to have their passports ready when they boarded Google's private jet.

The wedding was held in the Bahamas, and the ceremony took place on a sandbar in the ocean. Brin and his bride swam to the sandbar in bathing suits. Other guests arrived by boat.

Wojcicki grew up in Palo Alto. Her father is the head of Stanford's Department of Physics. Her mother teaches journalism at Palo Alto High School. Wojcicki cofounded the genetics and

THE SKY IS THE LIMIT

In 2008, Page and Brin, along with their wives, watched at California's Vandenberg Air Force Base as a satellite was launched into space. The satellite, displaying the Google logo, was part of an initiative at National Geospatial-Intelligence Agency. Google was entitled to exclusive commercial rights to all images captured by the GeoEye-1 satellite. Orbiting the Earth 15 times a day at a distance of 423 miles (681 km), the GeoEye-1 collected color images of the Earth and could capture 135,135 square miles (350,000 sq km) of images a day. This is an area larger than the entire state of New Mexico. The GeoEye-1 helped provide images of the Earth's surface for Google Earth.

In 2008, Brin placed a $5 million deposit with Space Adventures, a company that provided space shuttle missions to the International Space Station for private citizens. He planned to return to his native Russia in 2011 where a Space Adventures rocket would transport him into space. Brin and Page also agreed to build a new corporate complex at NASA's Ames Research Center, where they would partner with NASA on research projects.

biotechnology company 23andMe, which allows consumers to explore their own genetic information.

Later that year, Page also got married in the same region. On December 8, 2007, Page married longtime girlfriend Lucinda Southworth on Necker Island in the Caribbean. Page paid to fly in guests from around the world. He rented the entire island to keep the celebration private.

Southworth, who holds a PhD in biomedical informatics from Stanford, worked as a medical social worker in South Africa.

THE FUTURE FOR BRIN AND PAGE

In December 2008, the Brins welcomed a baby boy, Benji. The following November, the Pages became parents to a baby boy as well. Very little news circulated about the Google heirs, as Brin and Page have been diligent about protecting their privacy.

Google entered 2010 with stock shares selling at more than $600 each. On *Forbes*' 2010 list of the world's billionaires, Brin and Page shared the twenty-fourth spot, each worth $17.5 billion. Only eight Americans were wealthier than the Google guys, including Microsoft mogul Bill Gates.

AWARDS AND HONORS

Page was inducted into the National Academy of Engineering in February 2004, and both inventors were highlighted in *ABC World News Tonight's* "Persons of the Week." In November, the Marconi Society, which recognizes "lasting scientific contributions to human progress in the field of communications science and the Internet," named the duo Marconi fellows.[5] The society said of Brin and Page, "Their invention of a unique search engine technology fundamentally changed the way information is retrieved, by organizing much of the world's information and making it universally accessible."[6] And in 2005, both men were made fellows of the American Academy of Arts and Sciences. Page was given an honorary doctorate from the University of Michigan on May 2, 2009.

As new husbands and fathers, Sergey Brin and Larry Page had adventures yet to come in their personal lives. As the men looked to the future professionally, they seemed focused on making a difference in society. Says Brin:

As we go forward, I hope we're going to continue to use technology to make really big differences in how people live and work. . . . Obviously everyone wants to be successful, but I want to be looked back on as being very innovative, very trusted and ethical and ultimately making a big difference in the world.[4]

Page and his wife, Lucinda, keep their lives as private as possible.

THE IMPORTANCE
OF GOOGLE

O ver time, certain trademarked brand names
have become synonymous with the products
themselves, such as yo-yo, Frisbee, Xerox,
aspirin, and Kleenex. Just as someone might ask
for a Band-Aid instead of a bandage, a person now

commonly speaks of "googling" a topic instead of performing an online search for it.

Google has become part of everyday speech because it plays an important role in society. Not long ago, people relied on countless resources for information. Library books provided innumerable facts. Paper maps helped with making travel plans or determining the best route to a destination. Newspapers offered daily news. Photographs of entertainers, athletes, and other famous personalities were available in magazines or newspapers. Translating a sentence into another language required a dictionary or other language reference book. Finding a pizzeria required a telephone book. Although all of these resources have remained available, the information has become accessible with a few keystrokes on a computer using a single source: Google.

As Google grew and evolved, it revolutionized day-to-day life for computer users around the

GOOGLE TRANSLATOR

Google users have the option of limiting search results to Web pages written in their own language. However, they also have the option of utilizing another useful Google tool. Google Translate translates text from one language to another by simply inputting the text—users can upload documents or copy and paste the text from the original—and choosing the language the text should be translated to. Volunteer translators work to ensure the accuracy of translation of the 52 languages Google is currently capable of translating.

globe. They have come to rely on it for information, news, quotes, images, weather, maps, and much more. It has made information in countless resources easily searchable for its users. This easy access was not possible before the Internet, and it was still a complicated and unreliable process prior to Google's organization of Internet search results. All of these tasks would take a considerable amount of time without Google.

ADDICTED TO GOOGLE'S SPEED

Because Google has altered the way many people obtain information, there are some experts who argue it has changed the expectations the human brain has when seeking information. With a high-speed return of search results, users have grown used to immediate answers to search questions. Lengthy, in-depth reading of research topics might not seem as necessary as it

Google programs, including Google Earth, have changed the way people look for information.

once was. Users are able to click and browse through several linked Web sites quickly and often flit from one topic to the next.

A recent five-year study of online research habits performed by University College London reported:

> *People using the sites exhibited "a form of skimming activity," hopping from one source to another and rarely returning to any source they'd already visited. They typically read no more than*

one or two pages of an article or book before they would "bounce" out to another site. Sometimes they'd save a long article, but there's no evidence that they ever went back and actually read it.[2]

Nicholas Carr, a writer for the *Atlantic,* agreed that Google offers a wealth of online information, but he worried that the instantaneous search results and common surfing people do online might result in some negative side effects. He explained his new difficulty with reading books, which he blamed on his Internet use:

Now my concentration often starts to drift after two or three pages. . . . The deep reading that used to come naturally has become a struggle. I think I know what's going on. For more than a decade now, I've been spending a lot of time online,

"The faster we surf across the Web—the more links we click and pages we view—the more opportunities Google and other companies gain to collect information about us and to feed us advertisements. Most of the proprietors of the commercial Internet have a financial stake in collecting the crumbs of data we leave behind as we flit from link to link—the more crumbs, the better. The last thing these companies want is to encourage leisurely reading or slow, concentrated thought. It's in their economic interest to drive us to distraction."[3]

—Nicholas Carr, "Is Google Making Us Stupid?"

searching and surfing . . . My mind now expects to take in information the way the Net distributes it: in a swiftly moving stream of particles. Once I was a scuba diver in the sea of words. Now I zip along the surface like a guy on a Jet Ski.[4]

Since people have become accustomed to Google's ability to return lists of search results in only seconds, some experts worry that Internet users are losing the ability to find and read in-depth information.

This concern about how humans find and read in-depth information points to Google's influence. The search engine has forever changed how society thinks and acts when seeking information. Some have compared Page and Brin's contribution to humankind to the invention of the printing press, which allowed documents that once had to be copied

LIFE WITHOUT GOOGLE

In January 2008, Dr. Tara Brabazon, a professor of media studies at Brighton University in the United Kingdom, made news headlines when she banned her students from using Google and Wikipedia for research assignments. She explained that students "don't come to university to learn how to Google."[5] Instead, Brabazon provided her students with a list of more than 200 sources—mostly books and journals. She argued that students take everything found on the Internet as fact and end up ignoring "so many wonderful books [that] are published every day, providing the best research material in the world."[6]

GOOGLING TO DISTRACTION?

PBS *MediaShift* editor Jennifer Woodard Maderazo admitted in an article that she can barely remember how she performed research before the advent of Google and Wikipedia. Gone are the days of going to the library or opening a set of household encyclopedia books. She admits:

I haven't been to the library in about 10 years. I use the Internet for absolutely everything related to research, and in fact, I'd feel totally crippled without it. Google and Wikipedia have made me impatient and spoiled for instant infor- mation gratification, and the enjoyment of leisurely seeking has given way to an appetite for fast finding.[7]

Thanks to the Internet and such tools as Google and Wikipedia, online books, articles, and journals have replaced the need to walk into a library and locate printed sources in many cases. While a world with Google is much more convenient, some believe it is not an improvement, as Maderazo points out:

What you gain in speed of delivery you often lose in quality of information, not to mention the most intangible benefit of the way we used to get information: seek- ing it out slowly, wondering, theorizing, discovering, and feeling fulfilled in learn- ing. I miss that.[8]

by hand to be quickly reproduced and distributed. Google affects and simplifies the lives of millions of people worldwide every day.

GIVING UP CONTROL

The story of how two young prodigies forged a friendship and created the search engine known around the world is remarkable. Throughout their Google journey, Brin and Page insisted on following their instincts and doing things their way. Their willful approach paid off.

In November 2009, *Forbes* magazine named Brin and Page the fifth most powerful people in the world. The men held 59 percent of Google stock, allowing them to maintain the majority control of stockholders' voting power. However, in January 2010, they announced a four-year plan whereby they would sell 5 million stocks, bringing their share down to 48 percent. The two Google guys planned to give up majority control of Google by 2014.

WHAT LIES AHEAD?

Although Google endured its share of struggles, sometimes lacking money and sometimes facing legal battles, the company continued to expand and develop. The site delivers news, information, images, maps, videos, and e-mails to people around the world every day. At the heart of Google are Brin and Page, two computer scientists who believed they could craft a better method of organizing the world's Internet data.

The duo sees Google continuing to advance. "The ultimate search engine is something as smart as people—or smarter," Page explained. "For us, working on search is a way to work on artificial intelligence."[9] Brin agreed with his partner's thinking when he told *Newsweek* in 2004, "Certainly if you had all the world's information directly attached to your brain, or an artificial brain that was smarter than your brain, you'd be better off."[10]

While Brin and Page might not be thinking Google will one day outperform the complexity of the human brain, they do agree that today's search capabilities will seem very primitive in the future. Considering the immense growth Google applications have experienced in the last decade, the possibilities for the next ten years seem endless. In September 2010, the company introduced Google Instant, which produced suggestions and new search results with each letter the user types. This innovation promised to make searching faster than ever.

Regardless of how the inventors continue to advance their search engine, one thing is certain: Sergey Brin and Larry Page revolutionized society's quest for information with Google. Their contribution to history will be remembered as one that offers a vast amount of sorted and easily searchable knowledge at the world's fingertips. +

Brin and Page look forward to future developments in Google technology.

TIMELINE

1973

Lawrence Edward Page is born in East Lansing, Michigan, on March 26.

1973

Sergey Mikhailovich Brin is born in Moscow, Russia, on August 21.

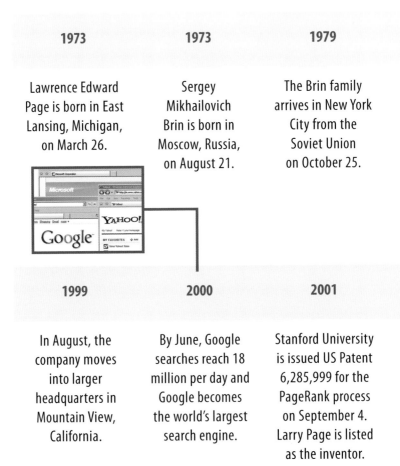

1979

The Brin family arrives in New York City from the Soviet Union on October 25.

1999

In August, the company moves into larger headquarters in Mountain View, California.

2000

By June, Google searches reach 18 million per day and Google becomes the world's largest search engine.

2001

Stanford University is issued US Patent 6,285,999 for the PageRank process on September 4. Larry Page is listed as the inventor.

1995

Brin and Page meet for the first time at Stanford University during Page's campus visit.

1996

Brin and Page work together on BackRub, the thesis project that would evolve into Google.

1998

Andy Bechtolsheim invests in Google, giving Brin and Page a check for $100,000 in August.

2001

Eric Schmidt is hired as Google's chief executive officer in August.

2002

In May, America Online (AOL) agrees to use Google's search program to reach its 34 million AOL users.

2004

Google launches its e-mail service, Gmail, in the spring.

TIMELINE

2004

Google moves to
its new Googleplex
campus in
Mountain View
in March.

2004

On August 19,
Google offers
stock for sale
to the public for
the first time.

2004

In August,
Brin and Page
announce plans
for Google.org, a
philanthropic arm
of Google Inc.

2007

Brin marries Anne
Wojcicki in the
Bahamas in May.

2007

Page marries
Lucinda
Southworth on
Necker Island
in December.

2008

Brin and his wife
welcome a son
in December.

2005

Google Maps and Google Earth are released.

2006

Google.cn debuts in China and becomes the most rigorously censored Google search engine.

2006

Google buys YouTube for $1.65 billion in October.

2009

Page and his wife welcome a son in November.

2009

In November, *Forbes* names Brin and Page the fifth most powerful people in the world.

2010

In January, Brin and Page announce a four-year plan to sell off stock and decrease their majority share of Google.

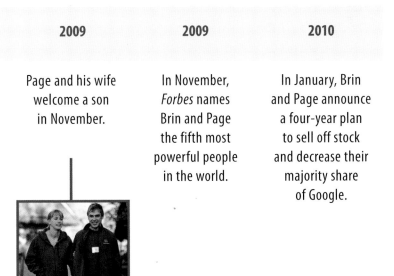

ESSENTIAL FACTS

CREATORS

Sergey Brin, August 21, 1973

Larry Page, March 26, 1973

DATE LAUNCHED

1998

CHALLENGES

Google had trouble making a profit before the company started selling advertisements in 2000 and hired CEO Eric Schmidt in 2001. Google has faced lawsuits over its bidding process for advertisement keywords. Google has also faced criticism over censorship in China and privacy issues related to Gmail and Google Maps.

SUCCESSES

Brin and Page created a search engine that was superior to its competitors. The company Google successfully turned Brin and Page's invention into a profit-making business. Google leads innovation in e-mail, maps, and many other online services.

IMPACT ON SOCIETY

Worldwide, millions of people use Google every day to search for information. Google has changed the way society expects to find and organize information. It has become so essential to modern communication that *google* is now a verb.

QUOTE

"Don't be evil."—*Google corporate motto*

GLOSSARY

algorithm
A complex mathematical equation.

angel investor
A person who invests his or her personal money in a start-up company.

anti-Semitism
Hostility toward or hatred of Jewish people.

citation
A reference to a published work.

cyberspace
The Internet.

encryption
A process of encoding text, making it unreadable to users for whom it is not intended.

entrepreneur
A person who starts or manages a business.

hyperlink
An electronic connection that takes a computer user to a new Web location by clicking.

Internet
A worldwide computer network.

PhD
Doctor of Philosophy, an advanced degree earned after a master's degree.

semiconductor
> A material that electricity can flow through; used in the making of computers.

silicon
> A natural element used in the making of semiconductors.

thesis
> A lengthy academic research paper written to attain an advanced degree.

URL
> The specific address of a web page on the World Wide Web, such as www.google.com; stands for Uniform Resource Locator.

Web crawler
> A computer program, often used by search engines, that scans Web pages, retrieves data, and returns it to a database.

World Wide Web
> A collection of hyperlinked documents residing on the Internet that appears as Web pages.

ADDITIONAL RESOURCES

SELECTED BIBLIOGRAPHY

Battelle, John. *The Search: How Google and Its Rival Rewrote the Rules of Business and Transformed Our Culture.* New York: Penguin, 2005. Print.

Brandt, Richard L. *Inside Larry and Sergey's Brain.* New York: Penguin, 2009. Print.

Lowe, Janet. *Google Speaks: Secrets of the World's Greatest Billionaire Entrepreneurs, Sergey Brin and Larry Page.* Hoboken, NJ: Wiley, 2009. Print.

Vise, David A. *The Google Story: Inside the Hottest Business Media and Technology Success of Our Time.* New York: Random House, 2005. Print.

FURTHER READINGS

Kallen, Stuart A. *Information Revolution.* Detroit, MI: Lucent, 2010. Print.

Stewart, Gail B. *Larry Page and Sergey Brin: The Google Guys.* Detroit, MI: KidHaven, 2008. Print.

Woodford, Chris. *History of Invention: Communications and Computers.* New York: Facts on File, 2004. Print.

WEB LINKS

To learn more about Google, visit ABDO Publishing Company online at **www.abdopublishing.com**. Web sites about Google are featured on our Book Links page. These links are routinely monitored and updated to provide the most current information available.

PLACES TO VISIT

Computer History Museum
1401 N Shoreline Boulevard, Mountain View, CA 94043
650-810-1010
www.computerhistory.org
Located in Silicon Valley, the Computer History Museum features exhibits on the people who invented and developed computers and related technology. The museum also features online exhibits.

National Museum of American History
1400 Constitution Avenue NW, Washington, DC 20004
202-633-1000
http://americanhistory.si.edu
The National Museum of American History, a part of the Smithsonian Institute, features exhibits about the role of science and technology in US history and daily life.

Original Google Headquarters
232 Santa Margarita Ave., Menlo Park, CA 95025
Although not open to the public, thousands of people travel to see the garage where Google began.

SOURCE NOTES

CHAPTER 1. HUMBLE BEGINNINGS

1. David A. Vise. *The Google Story: Inside the Hottest Business Media and Technology Success of Our Time.* New York: Random House, 2005. Print. 37.

2. Richard L. Brandt. *Inside Larry and Sergey's Brain.* New York: Penguin, 2009. Print. 41.

3. David A. Vise. *The Google Story: Inside the Hottest Business Media and Technology Success of Our Time.* New York: Random House, 2005. Print. 38.

CHAPTER 2. SERGEY BRIN

1. Mark Malseed. "The Story of Sergey Brin." *Moment.* Moment Magazine, Feb. 2007. Web. 12 Jan. 2010.

2. Ibid.

3. Ibid.

CHAPTER 3. LARRY PAGE

1. Janet Lowe. *Google Speaks: Secrets of the World's Greatest Billionaire Entrepreneurs, Sergey Brin and Larry Page.* Hoboken, NJ: Wiley, 2009. Print. 22–23.

2. David A. Vise. *The Google Story: Inside the Hottest Business Media and Technology Success of Our Time.* New York: Random House, 2005. Print. 24.

3. Andy Serwer. "Larry Page." *Fortune.* Cable News Network, 1 May 2008. Web. 12 Jan. 2010.

4. Janet Lowe. *Google Speaks: Secrets of the World's Greatest Billionaire Entrepreneurs, Sergey Brin and Larry Page.* Hoboken, NJ: Wiley, 2009. Print. 28–29.

5. "Sergey Brin and Larry Page." *Academy of Achievement.* American Academy of Achievement, 21 Mar. 2007. Web. 26 Dec. 2009.

CHAPTER 4. AN IDEA BECOMES REALITY

1. Mark Malseed. "The Story of Sergey Brin." *Moment.* Moment Magazine, Feb. 2007. Web. 12 Jan. 2010.

2. Janet Lowe. *Google Speaks: Secrets of the World's Greatest Billionaire Entrepreneurs, Sergey Brin and Larry Page.* Hoboken, NJ: Wiley, 2009. Print. 16.

3. David A. Vise. *The Google Story: Inside the Hottest Business Media and Technology Success of Our Time.* New York: Random House, 2005. Print. 40.

4. Ibid. 39.

5. Ibid. 39.

6. Ibid. 1.

CHAPTER 5. BUSINESS VENTURE

1. David A. Vise. *The Google Story: Inside the Hottest Business Media and Technology Success of Our Time.* New York: Random House, 2005. Print. 41.

2. Richard L. Brandt. *Inside Larry and Sergey's Brain.* New York: Penguin, 2009. Print. 72.

3. John Battelle. *The Search: How Google and Its Rival Rewrote the Rules of Business and Transformed Our Culture.* New York: Penguin, 2005. Print. 90.

4. Mark Malseed. "The Story of Sergey Brin." *Moment.* Moment Magazine, Feb. 2007. Web. 12 Jan. 2010.

5. "Google Milestones." *Google.* Google, n.d. Web. 26 Dec. 2009.

6. "Google's First Employee." *BBC.* BBC, 5 Sept. 2008. Web. 20 Jan. 2010.

7. Janet Lowe. *Google Speaks: Secrets of the World's Greatest Billionaire Entrepreneurs, Sergey Brin and Larry Page.* Hoboken, NJ: Wiley, 2009. Print. 93.

CHAPTER 6. MAKING A PROFIT

1. John Battelle. *The Search: How Google and Its Rival Rewrote the Rules of Business and Transformed Our Culture.* New York: Penguin, 2005. Print. 138.

2. Mark Malseed. "The Story of Sergey Brin." *Moment.* Moment Magazine, Feb. 2007. Web. 12 Jan. 2010.

3. Ibid.

SOURCE NOTES CONTINUED

4. Janet Lowe. *Google Speaks: Secrets of the World's Greatest Billionaire Entrepreneurs, Sergey Brin and Larry Page.* Hoboken, NJ: Wiley, 2009. Print. 93.

5. Richard L. Brandt. *Inside Larry and Sergey's Brain.* New York: Penguin, 2009. Print. 84.

6. "Google." *Oxford English Dictionary.* Oxford University Press, 2010. Web. 12 Jan. 2010.

7. "2002 Words of the Year." *American Dialect Society.* American Dialect Society, 13 Jan 2003. Web. 9 July 2010.

CHAPTER 7. GOOGLE GROWS UP

1. Richard L. Brandt. *Inside Larry and Sergey's Brain.* New York: Penguin, 2009. Print. 56.

2. David A. Vise. *The Google Story: Inside the Hottest Business Media and Technology Success of Our Time.* New York: Random House, 2005. Print. 132.

3. Richard L. Brandt. *Inside Larry and Sergey's Brain.* New York: Penguin, 2009. Print. 55.

CHAPTER 8. EXPANSION AND OPPOSITION

1. John Battelle. *The Search: How Google and Its Rival Rewrote the Rules of Business and Transformed Our Culture.* New York: Penguin, 2005. Print. 230.

2. Jean-Noël Jeanneney. *Google and the Myth of Universal Knowledge.* Trans. Teresa Lavender Fagan. Chicago, IL: University of Chicago Press, 2007. Print. 6–7.

3. "Google to Acquire YouTube for $1.65 Billion in Stock." *Google Press Center.* Google, 9 Oct. 2006. Web. 9 July 2010.

4. David A. *Vise. The Google Story: Inside the Hottest Business Media and Technology Success of Our Time.* New York: Random House, 2005. Print. 156.

5. Richard L. Brandt. *Inside Larry and Sergey's Brain.* New York: Penguin, 2009. Print. 141.

CHAPTER 9. THE BILLIONAIRE PHILANTHROPISTS

1. Larry Page. "Founders IPO Letter 2004." *Google Investor Relations.* Google, 2010. Web. 9 July 2010.

2. "What is Google.org?" *Google.org.* Google, 2010. Web. 9 July 2010.

3. Mark Malseed. "The Story of Sergey Brin." *Moment.* Moment Magazine, Feb. 2007. Web. 12 Jan. 2010.

4. Peter Jennings. "Persons of the Week: Larry Page and Sergey Brin." *ABC News.* ABC News Internet Ventures, 20 Feb. 2004. Web. 28 Mar. 2010.

5. "Google Milestones." *Google.* Google, n.d. Web. 26 Dec. 2009.

6. Marconi Society. "The Marconi Fellows." *The Marconi Society.* The Marconi Society, 2010. Web. 9 July 2010.

CHAPTER 10. THE IMPORTANCE OF GOOGLE

1. "Our Philosophy." *Google.* Google, 2010. Web. 9 July 2010.

2. Nicholas Carr. "Is Google Making Us Stupid?" *The Atlantic.* The Atlantic Monthly Group, July/August 2008. Web. 9 July 2010.

3. Ibid.

4. Ibid.

5. Jennifer Woodard Maderazo. "How Google, Wikipedia Have Changed Our Lives—For Better and Worse." *Mediashift.* Public Broadcasting Service, 25 Jan. 2008. Web. 9 July 2010.

6. Chris Arnot. "Tara Brabazon: Bowling Google a Googly." *guardian. co.uk.* Guardian News and Media Limited, 22 Jan. 2008. 9 July 2010.

7. Jennifer Woodard Maderazo. "How Google, Wikipedia Have Changed Our Lives—For Better and Worse." *Mediashift.* Public Broadcasting Service, 25 Jan. 2008. 9 July 2010.

8. Ibid.

9. Nicholas Carr. "Is Google Making Us Stupid?" *The Atlantic.* The Atlantic Monthly Group, July/August 2008. Web. 9 July 2010.

10. Steven Levy and Brad Stone. "All Eyes on Google." *International Editions on MSNBC.com.* msnbc.com. 12 April 2004. Web. 9 July 2010.

INDEX

ABOUT THE AUTHOR

Susan E. Hamen is a full-time editor who finds her most rewarding career experiences to be writing and editing children's books. She has written educational books on various topics, including the Wright brothers, the Lewis and Clark expedition, and Pearl Harbor. Hamen lives in Minnesota with her very supportive husband and two young, energetic children. She loves to spend her spare time reading, canning, sewing, or coaxing the family's persnickety orange tabby cat to show her some affection. Susan dedicates this book to her husband, Ryan.

PHOTO CREDITS